Wonders

Program Authors

Diane August

Donald R. Bear

Janice A. Dole

Jana Echevarria

Douglas Fisher

David Francis

Vicki Gibson

Jan Hasbrouck

Margaret Kilgo

Jay McTighe

Scott G. Paris

Timothy Shanahan

Josefina V. Tinajero

Mc
Graw
Hill
Education

Cover and Title pages: Nathan Love

www.mheonline.com/readingwonders

Send all inquiries to:
McGraw-Hill Education
2 Penn Plaza
New York, NY 10121

ISBN: 978-0-07-678205-5
MHID: 0-07-678205-0

Printed in the United States of America.

3 4 5 6 7 8 9 RMN 20 19 18 17 16

Unit 1 Take a New Step

The Big Idea: What can we learn when we try new things?

Essential Question

How can we get along with new friends?

Go Digital!

Come and Play

COLLABORATE

Talk About It

How are the children getting along?

Say the name of each picture.

Read Together

the

I can share **the** marbles.

We play in **the** sand.

I Can

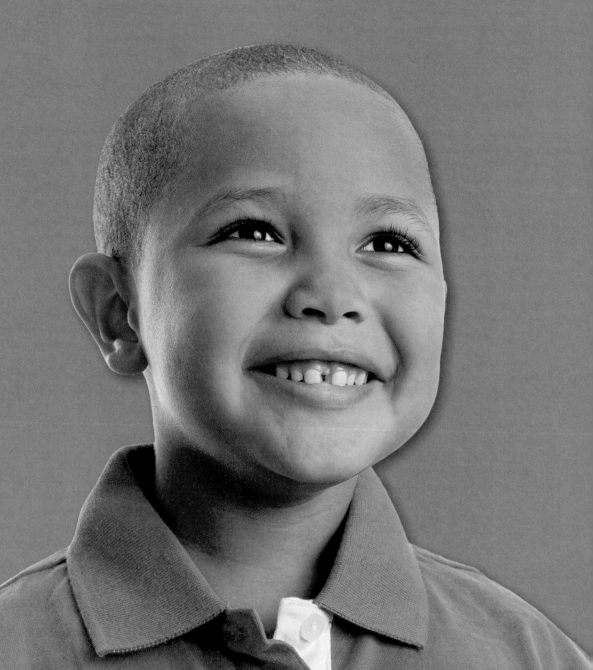

I can the .

see mitt

I can the .

see   mop

I can the .

see   drum

I can  the 🔵.
see   marbles

I can  the .
see　　　　　broom

Kyle Poling

Can I  the ?
see   map

Kyle Poling

I can.

Can I  the  ?

see   chair

17

Kyle Poling

I can.

I can  !

see me

19

Write About the Text

Hector

I responded to the prompt: **How are the marbles and the mop different?**

Student Model: *Informative Text*

The marbles are round.

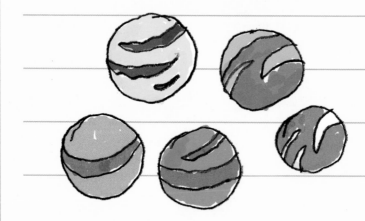

Describing Words

I used the word **round** to tell about the marbles.

The mop is long.

Your Turn COLLABORATE

How can the boy and a friend play with the things in the story?

Go Digital!
Write your response online.
Use your editing checklist.

Essential Question

How do baby animals move?

Go Digital!

22

On the Move

 Talk About It

How do penguins move?

23

Aa

Say the name of each picture.

Read the word.

 **am**

(t)Stockdisc/Punch Stock: Nathan Jarvis

we

We can hop.

We can see the animal.

We Can

We can .

walk

We can .

hop

We can .

climb

We can .

run

We can .

hug

I Can, We Can

I can  .
swim

We can .

swim

34

I can  .
fly

We can  .

fly

We can  .

run

Write About the Text

Pages 26–31

Katie

I responded to the prompt: **How are the tiger and the zebra the same?**

Student Model: *Informative Text*

The tiger has stripes.

Details
I used photo details to tell about the tiger.

Grammar

The word **zebra** is the name of an animal. It is a **noun.**

Compare

I told how the zebra is like the tiger.

The zebra has stripes.

COLLABORATE

Your Turn

What is the benefit of each animal's movement? Include evidence from the story.

Go Digital!
Write your response online.
Use your editing checklist.

Essential Question
How can your senses
help you learn?

Go Digital!

My Five Senses

Talk About It
How does the girl
use her senses?

Ss

Say the name of each picture.

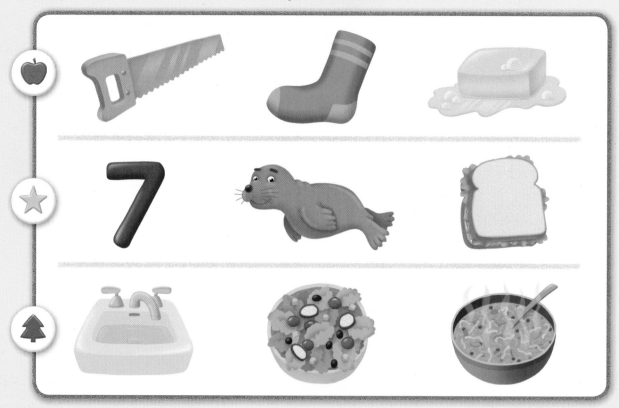

Read each word.

 am   **Sam**

(t) 97/E+/Getty Images; Nathan Jarvis

Read Together

see

I **see** Sam.

We can **see** the sun.

Sam Can See

We can **see** Sam.

Sofia Balzola

We can see the bird.

Sofia Balzola

Sam can see the .

bird

47

Sam can see the  .

bird

The  can see Sam.

bird

Sofía Balzola

I Can See

I can **see** the .
apple

51

I can .
touch

I can .
smell

(t) Oliver Rossi/Corbis; (c) McGraw-Hill Companies, Inc./Richard Hutchings, photographer; (b) Nancy Carlson

I can 👂.

hear

I can .
taste

Write About the Text

Sam Can See

We can **see** Sam.

Pages 44–49

Kim

I answered the prompt: **Tell what other senses the girl and her father might be using.**

Student Model: *Informative Text*

The girl smells flowers.

The father hears a bird.

Grammar

Nouns name things like **flowers.**

Clues

I used picture clues to figure out my answer.

Your Turn  COLLABORATE

Describe how Sam is using his other senses. What might he feel, smell, and hear?

Go Digital!
Write your response online.
Use your editing checklist.

Sappington Todd/Getty Images

56